THIS BOOK IS A GIFT

From

_____

To

_____

Date

_____

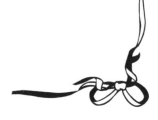

ENDORSEMENTS

"This devotional indeed will prepare a mind and heart to be ready for each new day, as it depicts that, in every situation of life, God's presence in one's life makes the difference. I encourage everyone who reads this devotional to approach it with an open heart to brighten their days without limit. A good work indeed."

—**'Wole Babalola,** CPA, MBA. CHMA
WT Babs Tax & Accounting Services Inc

"Having the correct mindset is one of the most important backbones for success. Being a web developer and consultant, I have dealt with a lot of people with the entrepreneurial spirit, and they seem to follow the pattern. This book lays out the path and mindset for success."

—**Eddie Vo,** CEO Ve-Studios LLC, Boston, Massachusetts

"This book is a library of great inspirations for successful living. I recommend it for anyone who wants to make a difference in life."

—**Johnson Folorunsho,** CEO of Johnson Inc, Boston, Massachusetts

"Charles Awodu is a living fulfillment of John 7:38, whose belly flows rivers of living waters, giving life to countless number of needy people. In his book, you will discover knowledge that would help build your life positively."

—**Apostle Dennis O. Ogbewi,** Grace Pasture International Christian Church, Boston, Massachusetts

"This book is an authority for the mind looking for solace in a confused state. It is an answered prayer to the mind looking for solutions in the midst of confusion. In a world where suicide has become a quick way to take souls away from the universe, this book will no doubt de-populate the evil world of suicide and agony. Reading this book has indeed been a blessing to me. I commend the effort of the writer."

—**Pastor Wale Odeyale**, Author of Faith as Universal Currency and The Colorful Marriage

"I have been privileged to have read through this book over and over and came to terms with these conclusions: The book is made for serious-minded persons desirous of high-level productivity for powerful results. You cannot apply the principles propounded in this book and remain without results; it's impossible. The book is a must-read for those aspiring to change in levels and noiseless breakthroughs. The book is useful to children, youth, and adults and can be read over and over. I recommend this book for results-oriented individuals who aspire for greatness."

—**Mr. Bukola Samuel Alabi,** President/CEO Bedrock Group

"The author was inspired by God to inspire others through this masterpiece. This book is value-loaded and useful to all and sundry irrespective of global region. Make every day of your life valuable with this book."

—**Pastor Comfort Alabi,** The Church of the Lord,
Kaduna South, Nigeria

"The tips in this book are mind-transforming guides for anyone who wants to make a positive attitude their lifestyle. I recommend this book for everyone who truly wants to leave an uncommon legacy for generations to come. A copy for each family member, friends, and, most especially, tomorrow leaders is a wise investment."

—**Ola Oladoja,** CEO Citipoint Realty Services, LLC,
Lynn, Massachusetts

101 GOLDEN TIPS
Making Your Day Count

101 GOLDEN TIPS
Making Your Day Count

CHARLES AWODU

Leadership coach/Public Speaker

Read, understand, and practice the contents of this book,
and make each day of your life a blessing to your generation.

EQUIP PRESS

Colorado Springs

101 GOLDEN TIPS
Making Your Day Count

101 Golden Tips: Making Your Day Count
Copyright © 2018, Charles Awodu

Published by Equip Press, Colorado Springs, CO

First Edition: 2018
101 Golden Tips / Charles Awodu
Paperback ISBN: 978-1-946453-49-5
eBook ISBN: 978-1-946453-50-1

EQUIP PRESS
Colorado Springs

ACKNOWLEDGEMENT

My acknowledgement goes to all pastors, leaders, teachers, professors, friends, family, and my parents, whose positive influence has shaped my life to keep seeing myself as a blessing and not a burden anywhere I found myself in life. I also appreciate my mother-in-law, Pastor Mrs. Comfort Alabi, who, during her stay when we had our twins, gave me an opportunity to maximize my vacation to write this book.

DEDICATION

To God, my family, and responsible future leaders.

THE AUTHOR

CHARLES AWODU is the President of World Leadership and Inspirational Foundation and Word of Light International. He is an insightful & internationally sought-after Leadership coach, teacher, and speaker in companies, churches, and social events. He hosts the program, 'Lighting the minds hour' in Massachusetts. He holds a Master of International Business Management degree and is currently pursuing post-graduate studies in Leadership at a leading university. He is a team member of the John Maxwell international leadership organization.

He is married to Olusola Awodu, a woman who has a deep passion for inspiring, teaching, and training children, and they are both blessed with four children—Peculiar, Excel, Wisdom, and Dominion.

FOREWORD

Success requires vision, action, planning, and strategy. Yet you cannot succeed without facing some challenges. True success requires resolution, reflection, and rational responses—and, above all, bringing God into what you do in order to be a product of success. Success is a practical, productive, and planning thing. So, someone can only celebrate true success when the God factor is brought into whatever he or she is doing or pursuing in life.

This book is a product of all the facts mentioned above. So, everyone who wants to succeed must make his days and years count in productive planning, reflective thinking, and profitable reading. Besides, a person must be godly minded, have a growth mindset, and not a fixed mindset.

This writer has demonstrated all the qualities emphasized above. Also, he has prepared this book with the mind to help others achieve success in life. The 101 Golden Tips have been carefully selected through the guidance of the Holy Spirit. Personally, I have grasped some salient things that can lead to productivity and great success in life in the course of reading through the book. That you have the book in your hand is a great privilege. So, read, and share it with others.

John B. Ajewole
Chief Editor
The Word of Life Ministries and Publications
Sango-Otta,
Ogun State,
Nigeria

INTRODUCTION

IT IS THE BRIGHTNESS of your mind that determines the brightness of your day, not the brightness of the sunshine. If the mind is dark, the day will look dull and dark no matter the intensity of the sun. The inspiration to write this book came from the account of creation, the first chapter of the Bible, and I believe that it will serve as the genesis for a new life to every intentional and committed reader. We saw from this chapter that God valued the power that each day carries as He focused productively on each day to create the whole universe within six days and rested on the seventh day, doing one thing per day to create the future we enjoy today.

Every day is a gift. To be alive to see a new day is a privilege not a right. The essence of every new day is for the accomplishment of a specific assignment for God and humanity. We are alive each day for a purpose; we must be conscious of this fact and be wise to apply our hearts unto wisdom, never wasting a second of our lives unproductively. Every second of our lives should count toward something of an excellent value. Time is life, and any second lost will require doubled efforts to be redeemed, or it will never be regained.

We must intentionally take advantage of each day as God did, if we want to live a productive life of impact that will serve as a reference for future generations. Every person's success and peace depends on how well he or she makes use of the day. Jim Rohn said, "You either run the day or the day runs you."

We all have an equal number of hours per day, but how well we maximize our days makes a big difference. Your hours per day are the best gifts you never paid for but which you have the freedom of choice to make count. You will never have today again in life, so make it count. Those who make their day count will be served by those who wasted theirs. Determine never to misuse each day from this day forward. Anything that wastes your day is your worst enemy.

As you proceed to study this book, pay close attention to the content of each tip for sound direction to make your day count. Congratulations in advance for making the decision to have a book like this as a guide to making each day of your life a blessing.

TIP 1

START EACH DAY WITH God. Oftentimes we put ourselves first by forgetting to acknowledge the goodness of God in allowing us to see another day. We behave as if it is our right, not knowing that there are richer or better people than us, who slept as we did the previous day, but never woke up to see the next. We expect superior results but neglect the source through which superior results spring daily. Never start any day without communicating with God as you are rising from your bed. Doing this daily is a way to refresh your mind and move positively into the day's activities with courage. Without God's leading, life is full of frustrations; and a life with Him is superior. Step out of your home daily with the mindset that you are never alone. **When God goes ahead of you, your victory is sure, because he never fails.**

Time is wealth, invest it.

TIP 2

HONOR GOD IN ALL of your accomplishments, and never take the glory that belongs to Him. Let it be in your heart that you have no power on your own to get anything meaningful done without His help. All ideas, energy, resources, and inspirations come from Him. If you want more, don't forget to give honor to the source from which you receive all things. Don't be too smart or wise in your own understanding. *Whatever you achieve today is just because of the life in you, and the controller of that life is God.*

Create your future today.

TIP 3

SET GOALS AND MAKE moves to hunt your goals. Don't sit down and expect miracles to happen. Daily plan the best ways to achieve your goals. It is good to have faith in God as believers, but God expects us to keep taking action in the direction of our goals. Faith without action is fake. We daily have parts to play to achieve success in life. We must take action if we want to have a change for the better in life. Take responsibility as you daily set your goals, and keep running with it until it is achieved. ***Your goal must be specific, measurable, achievable, and timebound. Let everything you do daily define your goal***.

Believe you can.

TIP 4

GUIDE YOUR TIME FROM time wasters. Your time can be wasted, used, or invested. Above-average people smartly invest their time each day; average people use their time each day; and below average people mostly waste their time each day. Don't give your time away; it is your life. Rather than spending time complaining, murmuring, or backbiting, invest it on something of value to make contributions that you will be remembered for. *Everything you spend your time on should have the potential to add value to your life and humanity. Blaming or gossiping does not.*

Success is in you.

TIP 5

FOCUS ON ONE THING at a time. Multitasking is good if you have the needed strength and power to engage it for a productive result. It becomes so useless when you multitask with no value or results to show for it. Your seconds should count toward something each day. It is not everybody who can multitask. It leads to the frustration of many. ***Strive daily to have something, at least one thing, to show for each day you spend.***

You can change the world.

TIP 6

START EACH DAY WITH a positive attitude. Nothing defines someone's future like a positive mentality; for as a man thinks, so he is. Our pattern of thinking will either make or mar our day. Your thoughts determine your take each day. Never give room for negativity in your mind as you wake up each day. *Anything that can make you unhappy in seconds has the capacity to spoil or mess up the following seconds, minutes, and possibly, if not checked on time, your entire day.*

Be a role model.

TIP 7

BELIEVE IN PRINCIPLES AND processes. Have the mentality that everything valuable in life has a process and principles that determine its value. This will help you to build lasting skills daily that have the potential to make you great in life. Those who hate principles and processes always lack the needed wisdom and endurance to sustain wealth in life. There is no shortcut to lasting success or victory in life. The process that leads to every end matters a lot not just the end. If the process is wrong or neglected the end will be wrong or deficient. Every organization has a culture, principles, and processes of achieving their goals; only those who understand this will find the place interesting enough to build their own future. *If you want to be intentional about becoming successful, get addicted to the principles and processes of success.*

Hate excuses.

TIP 8

BE SENSITIVE TO WHAT is happening around you. Some challenges or unexpected occurrences can benefit us or add value to our lives daily, but not everyone looks inward for the opportunities they carry. The solution to every problem is close to everyone but in disguise most of the time. We just need to be smart to recognize them. *There is something in every day to benefit you, for God loads each day with benefits. You must have a loving and sensitive spirit to enjoy this daily.*

Create your own sunshine.

TIP 9

HAVE A CAN-DO MINDSET. Don't just have a dream; have confidence in yourself, and trust God that you can do it. A lot of dreams die with the dreamers because they don't believe in themselves to pursue them. Achievement is impossible unless your mind can accommodate its possibility. **You can do anything if you believe in yourself and allow God's leadings to dominate all your daily plans.**

Strive for progress, not perfection.

TIP 10

DISCOVER YOUR PURPOSE FOR each day. Every new day is a great gift and privilege to advance your purpose in life. Ask yourself daily, *Why am I alive today? What have I to achieve and how and when do I need to achieve them?* Each time we fail to question our minds this way, the greater the chances are that we will waste that day. **A day is something that we can't stop from ticking away, so each day must be judiciously invested toward a purpose in life.**

Determine to rise.

TIP 11

DAILY SURROUND YOURSELF WITH people who have a positive mindset. Show me your friends, and I will tell you who you are. Some so-called friends can be highly toxic to your success in life. They take treasures away from your destiny through their negative influences. Sincerely speaking, not every friend can handle your success; some easily get threatened, disturbed, irritated, and envious of it. Be very selective in choosing friends at work and in your community. *A good friend brings clever, innovative, and promising ideas to the table for discussion—not gossiping or unproductive talk. They discuss solutions and never create problems. They help make your day count toward something of value.*

Start with what you have.

TIP 12

BE APPRECIATIVE. AN APPRECIATIVE heart is fertile ground for a fruitful life. It is ignorant to ask, *What is this little help you rendered?* Every bit of appreciation leads to further appreciation. Only the wise understand this. Never look down at anyone's effort in trying their best to assist you in your daily tasks, no matter your position in life. Lack of appreciation kills future opportunities, chances, or occasions to be helped. **Let your response lift the souls of your helpers every time. Their best may not be enough for you, yet learn to appreciate what they have to offer.**

Your only limit is you.

TIP 13

BELIEVE HUMAN BEINGS CAN change anytime. It is usually difficult to predict human behavior, so be mindfully prepared to move on with your life regardless of the changes you observe in people. When someone you are dealing with proves to be unstable, make moves to develop a Plan B. As everyday can never be the same, so also you should expect that everyone can't be the same every day. **Be proactive; never allow anything to dull or mess up your day.**

Do what makes you happy.

TIP 14

PREPARE TO BE HELPFUL daily. Rendering help to others within your capacity will surely add color to your day. There is a way an intentional helper feels after being able to successfully and positively touch someone's life with proof showing in the life of that person. They feel fulfilled and happy. *If offering help will make you unhappy, don't render it, because you will be hurting yourself terribly afterwards. You will begin to complain, murmur, and expect this person to be your subject in everything.*

Be kind always.

TIP 15

MAKE GOD YOUR SECURITY in all things daily. If you keep seeking security in a fellow man, or in your job, you will mortgage or lose control of your life to that person or that job. Seek God for divine security, and depend less on earthly security. While it is good to enjoy earthly securities, never allow your entire being to depend on them. It can be so deceptive, illusory, and misleading. ***Those who live to depend on job security hardly maximize or exploit their God-given potential. They live a life of limitations without impact.***

You can re-write your story.

TIP 16

DEVELOP A PRODUCTIVE PLANNING habit. He who fails to plan has planned to fail. Plan each day. It simplifies your efforts and makes accomplishments possible. Planning keeps you alive and sound. It is good to plan early to go far in life. Make short-, medium-, and long-term planning or preparations. It helps to boost your sense of commitment. ***Those who plan will be able see ahead. Plan well to live well***.

Focus on your goal.

TIP 17

PREPARE FOR OPPORTUNITIES DAILY. What distinguishes the poor and the wealthy or well-off people are the smarts to recognize opportunities and take quick advantage of them. Opportunities always come, and if we aren't mindfully expecting them daily, we can't see them. Have the mentality that anything great can happen anytime. *Every well-maximized opportunity will change your level to contribute more to society and boost your net worth.*

Don't doubt yourself.

TIP 18

NETWORK WITH LIKE-MINDED PEOPLE daily. A bird of a feather flocks together. Develop a good network in your area of calling or profession. This will help to boost your daily drive to move ahead in the chosen field or industry. Attend seminars, tutorials, and social gatherings to enhance your connections. A tree can't make a forest; it requires constant professional exchange of ideas from like minds to remain relevant in any field. Network to feed your mind with the right information to build your desired future. *Your ability to positively network from region to region regularly will bring about international exposure that can lead to a productive daily impact. Develop a global mindset for lasting relevance.*

Know who you are.

TIP 19

PARTICIPATE IN A MENTORING program. This is an avenue to tap into the knowledge of others who have gone ahead of you in any area of life. They give you a necessary guide for effective performance at work, home, church, or in the community. You stand a chance to be better if you are being mentored well. *Daily seek to stand on the shoulders of more experienced people in order to see far into the future.*

You are a blessing, not a burden.

TIP 20

CREATE AN IMAGE OF your future in your heart. We can only attain the future that we see deep down in our inner mind if we trust God for its fulfilment. Let the image of your desired future fill your heart and mind daily. It is the picture of your future that will keep driving you every second toward the attainment of your goals in life. We must have our destination in mind in our daily plans if we truly desire to get there. **Be very sure of who you want to be in the future, and keep working intentionally toward becoming it.**

Giving up is not an option.

TIP 21

BE COMMITTED TO LEARNING. The treasures of life are in books. Load your life with good books of great value. It will help to bring the best out of you to become someone people seek for knowledge. If you want to earn good profit or income, be ready to learn. *If you take away the letter "l" from the word "learn," what you will get is "earn." Make the habit of learning to earn, your daily lifestyle*.

Push yourself daily.

TIP 22

MAKE GOOD SACRIFICES. NOTHING good comes cheap in life. Anyone who wants to make his or her day count must be ready to sacrifice the needed resources for it. Never settle for an effortless way if you want to achieve something of excellent and terrific value. You have a part to play. God needs something in your hand through which he can multiply His blessings in your life. It is better to work with God to experience His daily blessings than waiting your whole life for a miracle. **Pay tomorrow's price today. ….we must do something exceptional to be distinguished from the crowd. The long lines for any cheap or less quality material is usually longer than lines for the expensive things; only the average people stay there to live within the common system of the world.**

You can do it.

TIP 23

LIVE YOUR DAY TO be remembered for good. If you want to be remembered in life or be in another man's memory tomorrow, make up your mind to be in their life today. It is God's expectation that we live to be a blessing to the world. Think beyond the size of your family. Think beyond the four walls of your church and community. Think about the problems waiting to be solved and strive to fill that gap for humanity. **What you plan to be remembered for tomorrow will determine what you will do today.**

Do your best daily.

TIP 24

DAILY EXAMINE YOUR LIFE. Each time you wake up in the morning or when you are going to bed, have a quiet time to re-examine yourself to see if you are on track to achieving your dream in life. You must be sincere to yourself, and make self-corrections where needed, it is expected that we daily add value. **When we daily draw our attention to the areas of our weaknesses for improvement, we stand the chance of having better ways of thinking to achieve our goals in life.**

Action changes things.

TIP 25

HAVE A WINNING AND "nevertheless" attitude. Life is full of challenges, and only those who show toughness in every circumstance can deliver significant and expressive results during tough times. You must possess a "nevertheless" character to overcome any battle that may come your way at any time. *No one prays for challenges, but having an inbuilt "nevertheless" mentality allows one to rule over the forces of life and live a life worthy of reference.*

Relationships are everything in life.

TIP 26

BE READY TO TAKE responsibility. Your life is your business. Face it consciously to make it count. It is only those who truly want to succeed beyond a limitation that decide to take responsibility for their future. A man who refuses to take responsibility for anything will surely end his life in frustration and emptiness. The fear to take responsibility is the reason for most frustrations, stagnations and oppressions. Taking responsibility is the shortest way out of poverty or lack. ***The inability to take responsibility makes one a liability or a beggar.***

Don't get distracted.

TIP 27

LET YOUR DAILY CONFESSION be superior to your condition. Your choice of words while going through the trials of life matters a lot. You must not give up deep inside while declaring a better tomorrow. Your confession and strength within must agree daily as you journey through challenges in life. ....declare your expectation daily instead of describing your situation to people. Some people have no solution but to add more problems Build your mind no matter how terrible your condition may be. Speak hopeful or positive words. **Confess positively, and keep taking bold and productive steps toward your goals in life.**

Passion drives perfection.

TIP 28

FORGET YOUR PAST. HOLDING on to your past interrupts the present and troubles your desired future. One thing about the past is that it is for a reference, not a residence. Negative experiences in the past are a weight that is capable of pulling you away from the opportunities before you. Until you detach yourself from the past, stagnation is inevitable. **It may be difficult, but everyone who wants to make an impact in life must never live in their past. It is impossible for a driver to keep looking behind and at time moving forward successfully. He must make a choice.**

No cost, no risk.

TIP 29

Spend wisely. Never borrow to please someone. The modern-day slavery is debt—especially for those who are not generating income. Go for what you need, not just what you want every day. Not all discounts are true discounts, and most store payment plans might be a long rope to draw, pull, or drag you into debt. *Develop serious hatred for any unproductive debt if you even have a reason to be indebted at all. Strive to daily live within your means. This will give you peace of mind to think productively toward your goals in life.*

Invest in yourself.

TIP 30

SAVE TO INVEST. THE common system of the world is that people live an average or below average life. No one can be richer than their employer except when they have another source of income—which would make them look foolish to continue as an employee. While working, learn to save and turn your savings into a profitable investment. *Until your resources begin to work for you, and not you working for your resources, others will continue to decide the extent of your impact in life.*

Your world is waiting for you.

TIP 31

DISCOVER YOUR PURPOSE. FIND a cause and live intentionally for it. Any man that is not living for a cause is like a man under a spell. Daily strive to find your purpose in life. The true power for an impactful life is in your purpose, but ignorance, fear, an unconcerned attitude, and a man-pleasing mentality can rob you of your purpose as designed by God. As you journey through each day, ask yourself, *Why am I here? What do I have a passion for? What can I contribute to life? What will I be remembered for after I leave?* When you begin to do something positive that you don't want to leave, you have possibly landed into your life purpose. Your purpose in life grows in phases. It has the capacity to spread from one point of focus. **You must be able to stand firm with conviction about your purpose, because nothing good comes cheap. Every treasure attracts a price for its prize.**

Arise and shine.

TIP 32

DAILY LEARN FROM CIRCUMSTANCES. Take advantage of learning something new with each day's events. There are lessons to learn from every circumstance whether good or bad, and in every day, there must be an experience that comes our way—either through our thinking or in our relationship with others. Learn from your mistakes, and don't look for ways to defend them. Be humble enough to be a productive learner, and never be the kind of a person who shifts blame to God and others. **Develop the consciousness that there is a gain in every challenge. Our challenges will certainly introduce us to change, either for better or worse, depending on our attitudes toward them.**

Time is limited, don't waste it.

TIP 33

BE ATTRACTIVE IN CHARACTER. Our behaviors speak much about our chances for success in our daily actions and pursuits. Learn to celebrate good things and the achievement of others if you want to be celebrated in life. Your destiny will attract what you celebrate. Our personalities are the first magnetic force that attract opportunities and success, not our education or background. Your degree(s) to some extent can land you a job, but it is your character that will sustain it. It is the quality of your character that defines the essence of your education. ***Wish others well as you strive for a better life, and don't be too envious of other people's progress in your move to succeed in life.***

Live your life & be happy.

TIP 34

KEEP ADDING VALUE. A person begins to stink, shrink, and diminish in thought and worth the moment they stop to positively increase the content of his heart and mind. If you see the need to go to school, or learn a trade, don't procrastinate. Action changes things, so act wise and fast. The best time to get anything done is today— tomorrow may be too late. ***Be proactive and sensitive to timing. Even though you may have graduated from a university, it does not prevent you from learning a new skill that could boost your opportunities for success and make you your own boss.***

Nothing works without effort.

TIP 35

BE SOLUTION MINDED. THE world needs solutions to problems and that is why you and I are here—as a solution bearer. Unfortunately, a larger percentage of people settled to be complainers, murmurers, whiners, objectors, protestors, and destroyers of good things. If everyone decides to solve a problem, the world will become a better place for all. Some can never see good in anything, yet with no better solution to offer. Our true prosperity is in the contribution we make to humanity. If we truly want to live a lasting legacy behind, let's strive to provide solutions to the problems facing humanity. **To make your day count, you must be that person who thinks and goes after solutions without creating problems for generations to come.**

Do nothing & will get nothing.

TIP 36

BE PRACTICAL IN YOUR belief. Let the expression of your belief positively affect others, starting with your family. We must be much more realistic and practical than theoretical. Practicing what you believe rather than teaching without demonstration will make a lasting imprint in the minds of people regarding how interesting your belief is. Don't limit kindness to the four walls of religious places. ***Show it as you teach, and let your impact be felt by your community as much as you can.***

Life is a race; overtaking is allowed.

TIP 37

BE QUICK TO HEAR, and slow to act. Be very fast to hear, but slow to respond. Let every response pass through an inner process before you react to any issue. Choose your words consciously before you release or spit them out. A word spoken is always difficult to reverse. Never allow anyone to push you into making rash decisions when you are not sure of anything. It is very easy to do something that will be everlastingly stupid when you are momentarily or temporarily angry or being challenged. ***Be very mature in your approach and responses every second. Let it be in your heart before you act.***

Keep the right company.

TIP 38

DON'T BE TOO RISK averse. Live to intentionally take calculated risks, for everything in life is a risk. He who is too afraid to take risks will never live an impactful life. Be very bold and courageous about making a good move to start anything you have conviction to make happen. All may not be perfect initially, but your courage will drive helpers your way. Don't fear mistakes. If mistakes happen, let the experience be the guide to the next trial. Just make sure that you are moving forward irrespective of your inability. Never live to be disappointed by what you don't accomplish even though you have the strength. Arise daily and dare to do the impossible. It is those who dare that deliver, not the cowards. ***Progress demands taking risk to face surmountable challenges. It is risky not to take risks.***

Never say it's impossible.

TIP 39

KNOW WHO YOU WANT to be. Have the picture of your desired future boldly imprinted in your heart and keep hunting for it. Create your world and rule in it. Not many people want to step ahead from where they used to be, even if they are complaining about it. We need to make a deliberate, thoughtful, and purposeful effort to change what we don't want in our lives. **Don't keep managing what you are criticizing and grumbling about in life. Resist them by actions and continue to hunt whom you want to be in life.**

Divine direction is superior to expertise.

TIP 40

BE THE LIGHT TO your world. Daily live an encouraging lifestyle through which someone can see light to walk successfully out of his or her darkness. Your gift is not given to you for only you but also for others. Develop a good mindset to positively brighten the hope of others. You will be directly and indirectly contributing to the betterment and advancement of the world when you are able to redirect someone from frustration to a successful or thriving path of life. Be an agent of hope and encouragement as you trip or journey through each day. *You are a light to nations. Don't hide the brightness of your light; let others see through it.*

Ignite the brain to work.

TIP 41

BE HOPEFUL. IT TAKES a hopeful mind to see the future, and a future you can't see, you can't experience. Don't be the type of person who gives up easily. No condition is permanent to those who keep their spirit alive in their darkest seasons. Keep believing and expecting the best from God while taking steps, no matter how small, toward your victory and success in life. Have the mentality that something good can happen at any time. Daily get ready in your mind for a positive change of status, and keep developing good relationships with others. ***Infuse your day with actions and a positive attitude every day. When there is life there is hope. Giving up is never an answer to any problem.***

Prepare for new opportunities daily.

TIP 42

DON'T BE TOO MIRACLE conscious. Faith without work is fake ....is a risk. You have a part to play for your success. Exercise the power that God has given you. If you depend so much on miracles every day, you may become too lazy to put your brain to work. It is better to do something good to attract God's daily blessings. Believe in miracles, but never live as if your whole life depends on it. The brain, eye, mind, ear, mouth, hands, and breath that God has blessed us with are for a specific purpose; use them well to activate daily miracles. **Some miracles will never come until eternity if you fail to do what's necessary. Every day is a miracle.**

You are your best & most trusted teacher.

TIP 43

MAKE BOLD DECLARATION. YOUR word powers your life. See possibility out of impossibilities. When the going gets tough, let your daily declaration keep you going. What you confess will eventually manifest itself. Your word is a seed that has the capacity to bear much fruit once it has been released to fertile ground. Get up from your bed daily and say, "I am a success; everything is working together for my good today. I shall not be disadvantaged or stranded in life. I am ending well today. All sensory organs in me are working in agreement henceforth. I am dominating my circumstance, and I shall not end in shame. I have a bright future." No matter the condition, let your confession be superior to your condition. ***Daily confession with action serves as a drive that leads to the manifestation of your heart's desires.***

Accept responsibility to avoid being a liability.

TIP 44

DON'T SETTLE FOR THE cheap path. The cheap path is a common path, and if you want to make a difference in life you must be ready to do uncommon things or follow a new path in a righteous manner. The cheap path is always good for average people and is usually longer. The way to remarkable success is expensive. Only those with the required currency can make the sacrifice for it. There is always a long line for cheap materials, and a lot of people can line up there until eternity. You can't settle for cheap ways to meaningfully fulfill a destiny. You must be very smart in spirit to recognize that you are an expensive asset who can't afford to mortgage his or her dream for a cheap price. *Do you know that not everyone that lines up for the annual Black Friday sales in the United States gets what they want after wasting their precious time? In fact, some could end up buying less quality products.*

Be faithful in small things.

TIP 45

DISCIPLINE YOUR MIND AGAINST offenses. If we live to interact with people, we can't avoid being offended from time to time, but training our mind to learn how to forgive in advance will empower us with the necessary ability to rule over the possible effects of taking offense. Life is too short to allow offenses to hold us back from maximizing the best of our days. One cannot see anything good in the life of a person who is seen as an offender until he or she forgives them. Holding on to offenses is a dangerous weight. *Imagine how unproductive a manager who had unresolvable quarrel on Monday's morning with the spouse or family member would be in office. Offences have capacity to limit our efficiency and effectiveness in life.*

Keep reaching out & touching lives.

TIP 46

SPEND QUALITY TIME WITH your family. Your family remains the most important company that you keep. Your job is secondary. Your presence will be much more rewarding than your presents, most times. It is a fact that if we create time to teach our kids the things that we learned later in life, they stand the chance of achieving greater things than us much earlier than we do. The time needed for our family cannot be replaced or swapped with money. We must strive to balance our relationships at home with our jobs. Both are important if we truly want to live a life of impact. Everything starts and ends with family. It is ignorant to pay less attention to our family because of anything else. *No matter how much we love our jobs, we will always have the need to be home.*

Godliness in character makes a great leader.

TIP 47

BE ALWAYS READY TO adapt to change. Change is a constant thing. No one hates it and lives a successful life. We must be able to guide our thinking to approach every trial and challenge with a positive attitude. Revival and different innovations or discoveries are taking place almost every second across the globe. Never get used to a way of life for too long. Be daily ready to adjust to better ways for improvement. As we are in the technology era, look for the means to move your business along and remain relevant in your industry. Globalization has taken over all aspects of life. ***Imagine a business that refuses to use computers because of their cost—how poor their delivery will look in the twenty-first century.***

If you want success. look for a problem to solve.

TIP 48

PAY ATTENTION TO CORRECTION. Those who love you will correct you repeatedly, because all sincere correction is usually difficult in an attempt to redirect us to a better path or solution and can be easily resisted the first time. Avail yourself to take a critical look at any correction you receive, to amend your ways where needed, to get better in whatever you are doing. We will always live to meet the need for good correction that we once resisted. Some corrections may be selfish in nature; nevertheless, set time aside to pay close attention to their contents before you consider them as irrelevant. *A man who refuses to avoid a reckless life possibly will end in frustration if he decides not to change.*

Only you can stop you.

TIP 49

HATE EXCUSES. EXCUSES KILL, destroy, and have every capability to steal opportunities. They can sentence anyone to everlasting stagnation. They are a self-limiting factor that hinder most people from fulfilling their destiny. Making excuses is a pattern of thinking that directs people to reject taking responsibility for their lives but instead to keep shifting blame to others—if possible, God or Satan. *Imagine a man at the age of ninety-eight years old who is still blaming his father for being poor. It is indeed a serious matter!*

No one knows everything.

TIP 50

AVOID PRETENSE. PRETENDING TO be someone you are not is a serious ignorance of the reason you were created. Living a life of pretense gives room for you to be taken advantage of by wicked people. Do not settle to be a "yes" person. Learn to boldly say no when necessary. You have your life to live, and to make it count, you must be you. Anyone who is full of pretense hardly has peace deep in their innermost mind. There is always something to hide from another person; they never have freedom to live their true potential. To make your day count, you must avoid self-limiting characteristics, like pretense. *A man who has money but refuses to enjoy it so that people will not talk is surely saving it for people who never sweat for his wealth.*

Hopelessness is an evil weapon, resist it.

TIP 51

GUARD YOUR INTEGRITY. THE forces of life most of the time push people to rule out integrity from every relationship. Do the right thing in your best interest, and never allow greed, or a move to acquire wealth, to overshadow right judgement any day. Integrity will speak for you where money makes no sense. Many people fail in the future because of an inordinate drive to acquire wealth and popularity today. Integrity is the pillar upon which enduring success is established. Build integrity if you want to have prosperity with lasting peace. Do all you can never to compromise standards for anything. ***A corrupt believer is a disgrace to God's kingdom and humanity. Be a good ambassador always. Be careful when people say, 'this is business, this politics or this is family affairs. Let your conscience play a good role.***

Add value daily.

TIP 52

DESPISE NOT YOUR LITTLE beginnings. Nothing that is big starts big. We must learn to start off everything with the little we have and keep tendering it to maturity or plenty. There is always a time to think, plan, grow, and keep growing to get there. There is a greater harvest in every seed if it can be planted and nurtured to grow. Never overlook the little you have by looking at the accomplishments of those who have gone ahead of you. Appreciate whatever you have and be very committed, and someday you too will become a point of reference. Everything is a process; be patient to follow through. ***Anyone that thinks he has no resources to start a business should ask himself if he has an eye, mind, ear, leg, hands, and brain, for these are the basic capital that one needs to start anything in life.***

Keep on moving on!

TIP 53

DON'T BELIEVE IN LIMITATIONS. Those who believe in limitations never go far in life. Be ready to go the extra mile. No successful achiever believes in limitation. The circumstances of life will always present limits for men, but those who disregard man made definitions and limits always enjoy a ceaseless flow of God's grace to drive their dreams to fulfillment. Have the mindset that your success in life is in your best interest, and you can't just accept any roadblock as the final stop. The sky is the starting point for those who understand God's plan for their lives. You can live beyond limits. You are the only person who can limit yourself. No one is born with the mindset of limitations; we grow into it by influence. *A man who believes that he cannot achieve something will never try, and if he tries, his mindset might make him fail.*

Time is wealth, invest it.

TIP 54

LOOK FOR THE FACTS. A lot of relationships have been destroyed and thousands of business opportunities and ideas lost due to wrong assumptions. Daily seek understanding rather than assuming what you can't defend. Don't take gossiping as fact until you personally get the right information. Most times people seek to destroy others to enjoy selfish favor from you. Don't waste your valuable time with gossipers; be very wary of them if you want to live a fulfilled day of life. *A staff or colleague who fails to correct other friends but instead comes to you to discuss them might be looking for avenue to gain undue favor from you.*

Create your future today.

TIP 55

DAILY LEAD ALONGSIDE OTHERS. Leading with other people enhances the mutual growth of a group of people. It gives a sense of belonging to the people and boosts productivity. It helps to simplify the day's task because everyone will naturally strive to do their part to accomplish a common goal. It will help you to inject leadership traits into the people that will be responsible for building up quality people to surround you for excellent achievement. *A leader that is too authoritative hardly gets sincere and committed followers*.

Believe you can.

TIP 56

Avoid procrastination. Don't defer or postpone what you have time to achieve now. You never can tell what will happen tomorrow. Develop the mindset of "do it now." This will afford you the ability to maximize your time. Set your priorities right for each day according to your goals. Learn to tackle most difficult jobs as early as possible to enjoy your day. One of the major causes of procrastination is the fear of failure. *A person who keeps deferring to go back to school while unmarried may never do so when he or she begins to raise children.*

Success is in you.

TIP 57

LEARN LESSONS FROM CHALLENGES. Life is full of challenges, and no one is immune to it. Challenges build those with positive attitudes and sinks those with negative mindsets. In every pain there are gains, but it takes the grace of God to see them. Every challenge is to teach us a lesson for future reference. Most often challenges introduces us to others or possible change depending on our mindset. ***Challenges will either bring fear or courage to define the extents of our influence in life.***

You can change the world.

TIP 58

VALUE YOUR TIME. TIME never expires in itself, it is of same 24hours forever but it is we human beings that keeps expiring as each day passes by. You don't need to waste your time on things that bring you no reward. Concentrate your energy on things that add value to your day to achieve your set down goals. Any second of unproductive discussion is a great waste. Convert every opportunity of time to boost your chances for success each day. Time wasters live to regret their tomorrow. ***Show me a man who values every second of his time, and I will show you a potential achiever of tomorrow.***

Be a role model.

TIP 59

BE REAL. BE YOU in all you do because that is the surest way to peace of mind. Never pretend to be humble when you know the right thing to do. Be very rational in your attitude. Pretense is a form of self-torture, punishment, and deceit. It has the strength to limit a destiny never to make an impact in life. Pretense will blind your understanding from knowing your worth. It may be very costly to live out who you are, but note that the gain is far better than pretense. ***A man who discovers the right way to go but refuses to take that step because of a possible reaction of his boss or someone else will live to meet his ignorance.***

Hate excuses.

TIP 60

BE FAITHFUL. A LIFE of deceit is a life of shame and frustration. Value every position of trust and never block your future benefits and relationships for temporal gain. We live in a very small world, and sometimes our past deeds stand to question our future opportunities. If you are holding a public post, let it be in your mind that the public post is a public trust. Let people find you always faithful in all things. **An officer who is misusing the organizational resources is destroying the chances to employ more employees and reduce the rate of unemployment.**

Create your own sunshine.

TIP 61

LOOK FOR A PROBLEM to solve. The secret of prosperity is in the ability to solve a problem. You need to either render a service or produce goods to meet the needs of people. If the earth remains, problems will ever be. Ask yourself, *What problem have I to solve?* Anyone who thinks that God will come to physically meet their needs will wait until eternity. **God expects us to make moves daily toward our goal. True and lasting success or prosperity is in our ability to make productive contribution towards solving a problem in the community, organization or in the world.**

Strive for progress, not perfection.

TIP 62

PUT IN YOUR BEST at what you do every day. Live an intentional life and strive for excellence in all you do. Everybody loves excellence but not everybody can make excellent services or product. Excellence attracts reward and recognitions. Aim at it always in whatever you do. Avoid the habit of doing things halfway. It is an act of excellence which distinguishes the successful people. Anything done excellently has the chance to announce us in life. Excellence is so hard to find, yet it is the key to uncommon success. Plan and pray before you start anything and keep improving on it. Be very committed to your goal. Develop a mentality that your success is in your best interest. *A student that put his best into his or her studies will surely attain outstanding success.*

Determine to rise.

TIP 63

BE CONSCIOUS OF YOUR time. Time is life, and it can easily be wasted in ignorance. Plan and follow through with your plans on time. Learn to adequately manage your time, and don't squander it with those who have no plans. Success awaits anyone who uses his time productively. Don't spend your time playing games or watching television every day, convert it value or product. There should be a time to work and time to play. Time is highly limited; keep track of it to make your life count. ***The life of an old person who wasted his or her time at a youthful age is always full of regrets—of what they could have done with their time. Make moves to make an impact when there is power and time.***

Start with what you have.

TIP 64

TAKE RESPONSIBILITY. AS AN adult, it is ignorant to keep blaming anyone for your failures or circumstances in life. Decide to take charge of your life as given by God. Never put the responsibility of managing your life to someone else. In fact, God wants you to play your own part if you want to live a life of impact on Earth. *Only those who sincerely love to live take responsibilities. You cannot avoid your responsibility today and not have reason to blame others tomorrow.*

Your only limit is you.

TIP 65

LEARN FROM RESPONSIBLE ADULTS. It is not every adult that has something good to offer. Some are terribly empty and dangerous to relate with. A responsible adult will have a good conscience, the fear of God, and proof of their labor. Everything about them will inspire you to do better in life. Be very selective in choosing which adults mentor you toward achieving a goal. ***Those who have gone ahead have experiences from which we can learn early to become better than them in no time.***

Do what makes you happy.

TIP 66

WORK HARD AND THINK smart. Working hard is good, but thinking smart brings about quick and excellent results or rewards. Laziness leads to penury, and all hard and smart work with the fear of God brings profit. Some prefer not to work but love to earn. Learn to earn. You need to exercise your body either to think productively or engage in physical labor in exchange for monetary value. Don't always settle for free things. Expecting help from others and not striving to help others limits the extent of our impact. Receiving things for free prevents us from believing that we can help others achieve great things. You are an asset not a liability. Daily think of what you can contribute to help others and the growth of the economy. **Nothing builds the economy like the hard and smart work of the citizens. Be a global builder.**

Be kind always.

TIP 67

Pursue your vision with action. An idea or vision remains useless if it is not birthed. What brings a vision into fruition is a chain of action. The moment you conceive of an idea, get enslaved to it. As you go deeper into a vision that is a service to others, you will begin to attract people who will support you to drive the vision. But if you do not make a move, the idea or vision will die at the point of conception. *A vision not pursued is a future being destroyed.*

You can re-write your story.

TIP 68

Seek right information. Valuable information is the currency of destiny. It directs a person or group to success and victory faster and without much effort. Attend good seminars and read books written by great minds. It is the lack of relevant information which makes accomplishing a set goals impossible or difficult. Useful information is a strong and convincing driver of success. If many who have given up in their pursuits in life could seek right information early for sound direction, they would never have given up. ***It is a wise thing to seek God's daily counsel for direction and to learn from others who have gone ahead of us in life.***

Focus on your goal.

TIP 69

BE COURAGEOUS. BECAUSE OF the fear of what could go wrong, many people never live to fulfill their destiny or try to pursue a worthwhile goal throughout their lifetime. What a waste of potential! Everyone needs courage to attain success in life. Life is full of challenges, and you can only dare to deliver if you are daring or bold enough to run through your daily activities with confidence. Internal and external oppositions to be conquered will always be there. Anyone can have a vision, but it is those who have confidence in themselves and trust God that can make a vision a reality. Anyone who is too scared to take a risk can never live an impactful life. **Your success in life depends on the extent of the risks you are ready to take. It is risky not to take risks.**

Don't doubt yourself.

TIP 70

Don't over-celebrate past success. Appreciate past accomplishments but never stop there. Keep reaching out for a new level. Talking or testifying about what you achieved years ago, repeatedly without thinking of stepping forward to advance on it or do something new, is a great force or sign of stagnation. *A top graduating student ten years ago who refuses to add new value to him or herself might become the employee or servant of the worst graduating students from the same year—those who keep adding value as each day passes by. Keep on moving on!*

Know who you are.

TIP 71

RESOLVE DISPUTES EARLY. DISAGREEMENTS are inevitable as we relate with others and journey through life here on Earth. Misunderstandings and mix-ups will come but be wise to clear them up so as not to mess up your next moment or day. Any unsettled disagreement can destroy many prospects, and one disappointing or upsetting day can multiply into countless days or years if we fail to resolve it and move on. Do all you can to make sure that you are at peace deep within your mind and seek for peace with others. *A lot of fear, misunderstanding, and wickedness of one against the other is because of past seeds of discord that were planted and keep growing from generation to generation in the family, community, and among nations.*

You are a blessing, not a burden.

TIP 72

BE COMMITTED TO YOUR dream. Do what you believe in and be prepared to make the needful sacrifices to bring your dream into manifestation. Every dream has the tendency to attract oppositions; have this understanding in mind before you start to pursue any goal. The undisputable dislike of many may not be because of who you are but because of your decision to make a difference in life. If you have this understanding, you will never see any opposition as a threat but as a reason to move on with your dream in order to prove the doubters wrong and be a blessing to your world in the long run. *Commitment is the key to unlock the hidden treasures of any dream.*

Giving up is not an option.

TIP 73

LEARN TO REVIEW YOUR day's activities. At the end of each day's job, ask yourself, *What have I gained today?* You should have a reward for the resources you have invested into your day. The time you spent that cannot be regained, foods you eat that have digested, and other forgone alternatives demand that you get proof of what you have spent your day on. This pattern of thinking will boost your positive results in life. **Anyone that ate in the morning before going to work or school should be able to question the essence of his or her breakfast or lunch at the end of the day.**

Push yourself daily.

TIP 74

KEEP GOOD RECORDS. IT is most beneficial to keep track of your activities for future reference. The procedure that leads to any accomplishment is worth tracking. It will be good for you or someone in the future because it offers the direction of your operations or activities. Every good record is proof of past efforts. It enhances accountability which encourages doing better and being in good standings with the relevant laws of the land. *A lack of good record keeping is the reason for frustration for most people and organizations or groups of people.*

You can do it.

TIP 75

LIVE UP TO YOUR promise. It is better not to promise at all than to promise and not fulfill it. Be very sure of the means to fulfill every obligation. Your ability to keep your promise dictates the level of respect your partners will have for you in any business dealings, or in life, generally. It is one of the yardsticks by which to measure your integrity. A bad promise keeper is a dangerous friend to keep. If you cannot live up to your promises due to unforeseen events, let the reason be known to your partners and that will add more respect to you than keeping silent. ***A broken promise can lead to the disarray of someone's life or destroy the trust that could earn you success in future. If you care for your future, and that of your friend, think deep before you make a promise for anything***.

Do your best daily.

TIP 76

THINK ABOUT CONTRIBUTING TO life. Some people have the mindset of taking from people and their society but never think about making a contribution to anything. They have the "taking" mentality that limits them to a spot without knowing. Only those who contribute have the opportunity to rule their world. If you don't want to end in frustration, think contribution. Learn to contribute to your communities if you don't want to live like a slave or beggar. Everyone has something to contribute if we care to discover it. Selfish people will never think about making a contribution, and that is why they hardly make an impact in life. *Your lasting prosperity is in your contributions—the service you render or products you make available to solve a problem. Contribution is in sizes and that's why the reward of an employer and the employees will never be the same. Think! No employee can be richer than his employer.*

Action changes things.

TIP 77

DAILY MOVE TO CREATE your desired future. You don't walk into the future; you must create it. Many people pray daily for a prosperous future thinking that God will come down to move them into that future without doing their own part. This set of individuals will never work with the ideas or opportunities that keep coming their way to make that future a reality. Faith without work is fake. Think, plan, and act fast to create your desired future. **Anyone who keeps making year-to-year resolutions without action will become a serious burden to himself and the people around him or her tomorrow.**

Relationships are everything in life.

TIP 78

EXPRESS YOURSELF BOLDLY. A closed mind or mouth is a closed destiny. Be bold to make your intention known at all times, and refuse to die in silence. Some wicked people take advantage of silence at the detriment of people. What you don't want, you don't watch. Be confident to say no to whatever you don't want. Having this quality will help you to maximize your full potential and rule in life. *A lion is never the biggest or fastest animal in the bush, but its boldness makes him the ruler of all.*

Don't get distracted.

TIP 79

NETWORK WITH POSITIVE THINKERS. Networking in this globalization era is the fastest means to drive your vision and make your presence known to the world. Don't keep your vision hidden. Daily seek to network with people who have common goals in order to increase your net worth. Your presence can be in far-away places without you being there in person. Take advantage of information technology, particularly social media, in addition to your one-on-one or group connections. ***If you are not networking, you are not working, so network to be a blessing to your world as expected by God. "Ye are blessings to nations."***

Passion drives perfection.

TIP 80

DON'T WAIT FOR A perfect time. There isn't a day when everything will be perfect. Dare to start and you will begin to walk toward perfection. Passion drives perfection, and it is sufficient to bring your heart's desires to fulfillment. The right time is right now; if that idea is in you, move into action now. It is action that changes things. If not, the wind might blow it away from your mind. There are always winds of life which blow every second to catch up with those who are waiting for the perfect conditions to initiate their ideas. *A man who keeps waiting for the perfect conditions to do something might end up not doing anything in life. Act with speed to birth your ideas.*

No cost, no risk.

TIP 81

RESPECT CONSTITUTED AUTHORITY. EVERY society is powered by an enabling law set down to make life better for all. You can't respect the laws that guide any organization or country and fall victim to its penalty. Disobedience to the law can lead to a severe punishment capable of destroying your reputation or limiting the extent of your impact in life. Law is the foundation of orderliness, and orderliness leads to peace and harmony in society. *It will take an arduous work and proof beyond a reasonable doubt for a man being jailed for corrupt practices to hold a public post in any society where there is an absolute respect for law and order. If you believe in the possibility of a better future, let respect for the law be your daily guide.*

Invest in yourself.

TIP 82

SEEK BETTER WAYS. INSTEAD of condemning the systems that have been in place, look for better ways to advance on their weaknesses. Such a system might have been the best at the time that it was instituted. You will make a greater impact by daily engaging in those things that can complement or are capable of gradually wiping away the old system rather than destroying it without offering solutions to make it better. Be solution minded every second rather than finding fault without reason. *If the best of someone is not good enough for you, what else do you expect from him or her than to make a step to advance from where he or she stopped?*

Your world is waiting for you.

TIP 83

BE A GOOD LEADER. A good leader cares for the wellness of their followers, and often seek to get feedback for improvement. They lead with people in order to duplicate themselves. Every act of good leadership that your team enjoys daily will influence them for better productivity. Manage every resource at your disposal effectively and efficiently to improve the standard of life of your employees, team, or citizens. An impactful leader is the one who can provide needed inspiration to his team to reach a higher altitude in life. *A successful leader is the person who can raise someone to perform better than himself after his departure*.

Arise and shine.

TIP 84

ENCOURAGE COURAGE. THE BEST way to be in someone's memory is to be in his life today. Never wait to see someone's success before encouraging them. Encourage them because you can envision their success. Some people just need a little courage to be who God has created them to be. Everybody needs encouragement and one act from us can be just what someone needs. Always speak encouragement to people in the organization where you work or to people around you. Be very positive in all your dealings. A candle loses nothing for lighting others. *Anyone who encourages others to succeed today might directly or indirectly benefit from the seed of courage that they planted.*

Time is limited, don't waste it.

TIP 85

PLANT A GOOD LEGACY. Think and work for the things you want to be remembered for after your tenure is over or when you are no more. Only those who are cognizant of what they will be remembered for will do good while holding a position or while living on earth. A surviving legacy is not truly in structures but in the value of the knowledge that you imparted onto others for generational influence. ***Anyone who considered that having several houses or businesses for their children is the best legacy, should know that the character to manage such an investment is the real legacy that he or she needs to lay emphasis on.***

Live your life & be happy.

TIP 86

LOCATE THE RIGHT ENVIRONMENT for your dream. Not all soil is good enough to plant every seed. Some soil needs fertilizer, and for some, no matter the amount of soil booster that you apply, seeds just won't grow on it due to harsh weather conditions. No matter what you do in the wrong environment, getting meaningful results will be difficult. Seek to grow your ideas or career in the right environment and strive to discipline yourself to make the best use of it to be a blessing to your world. **Dream killers will always exist because dreams naturally attract coldheartedness and envy.**

Nothing works without effort.

TIP 87

SET ATTAINABLE GOALS. SETTING unattainable goals for any day is the shortest way to frustration and a waste of resources throughout the day. Your goal must be specific, measurable, attainable, realistic and time bound. Create short-, medium-, and long-term goals and keep moving in that direction each day. Attainable goals keep your spirit alive and in the right attitude to achieve it. Simplify your process to make achievements possible. *It is those people who understand the importance of time that will care to set achievable goals for each day of their lives.*

Do nothing & will get nothing.

TIP 88

BE HUMBLE BUT DON'T be unwise. Every boss appreciates working with humble people daily but not every one of them is humble enough to respect the humility of their subordinates. Some are dangerously wicked, taking humility as a weakness and an opportunity to present to others what they can't accept from anyone. Humility does not mean that you go with every proposition; at times you must resist some. *Your resistance to some selfish propositions could be taken as disobedience, but remember you can't sell yourself cheaply if you want to make your day count. You must be you.*

Life is a race; overtaking is allowed.

TIP 89

DON'T DISCUSS YOUR SECRET with your competitors. Your secret is your strength to make an impact in life. Never be too careless to let it out to others. Competitors daily look for an opportunity to take advantage of suppressing and muffling your growth. *Be very wise not to trade your power of influence for anything. Your secret is your pride by which you work to make a difference in life.*

Keep the right company.

TIP 90

BE REAL TO YOURSELF. Let your yes be yes, and your no be no, for anything outside this is from the devil to oppress and limit you from fulfilling your dream in life. When you make a mistake, admit it. Be very fearless to say the truth and let your conscience guide you daily. Don't allow the system of this world to force or trick you to live in pretense. It is very harmful to the survival of any destiny. ***A man who listens to the negative opinions of the people will daily find it difficult to live a life of difference.***

Never say it's impossible.

TIP 91

Be teachable. Having a teachable character gives you the opportunity to grow better and faster in life. Everyone has the chance or possibility to learn from others each day as we relate or interact. Listen to learn first, and let your response spring from the lesson you learned from your interaction or conversation with others. Wise men do not lack a teachable spirit. ***Every successful leader possesses a teachable heart.***

Divine direction is superior to expertise.

TIP 92

THINK BEFORE YOU ACT. Don't be in haste to react to issues. Avail yourself a reasonable amount of time to think and make adequate plans before you act on any critical issue. You stand to lose credibility when taking the wrong actions becomes your identity. Don't allow people to rush you into making decisions when you are in doubt of being able to keep your promise. *It can be very difficult at times to reverse an action already committed, but if you are still in the process of it, you can easily change it. However, this should not lead us into procrastination.*

Ignite the brain to work.

TIP 93

DAILY PUT YOUR BRAIN to work. To keep multiplying your contributions and impact in life, your brain must be at work. There can be no valuable gains without a working brain. God designed the brain to serve thinking and coordinating purposes, and we must use it productively to give honor to God and blessings to humanity. No one suffers drain when the brain is effectively put to work. Idle thoughts are a product of an idle brain. **The best strategy to keep your brain working is to keep productively exercising it daily.**

Prepare for new opportunities daily.

TIP 94

DON'T BE ASHAMED OF what is gainful. At times things that lead to success can be so unattractive at first sight or discovery, but if you have conviction in yourself, never mind the look and just go ahead. People may laugh at you for following such a path. Some experiences that bring about an excellent result might be tough and rough but the potential that they carry might be much more rewarding than those that appear easy at the start. Be ready to pay the price of greatness if you want to make a difference in life. **A wise man looks at the prize not the price. They consider every price of greatness as normal and nothing less.**

You are your best & most trusted teacher.

TIP 95

HUNT FOR FEEDBACK. GETTING and working on feedback from people is the best way to enhance your capacity to reach your desired goal and increase the intensity of your impact in life. Expect feedback from others daily. It could be positive or negative; appreciate it because the essence of feedback is to keep improving daily on whatever you are doing. Only a leader that set for a failure will always want people to give him or her a positive feedback. There is always a room for improvement. **Be very objective about feedback and treat them as your daily breakfast as a leader.**

Accept responsibility to avoid being a liability.

TIP 96

BE DISCIPLINED. THE ACT of sound discipline must not be taken as punishment. Discipline helps to limit excesses and unproductiveness. It narrows the wise minds toward a specific goal daily. It makes people enjoy the pains of tomorrow today. Without discipline, no one can live a meaningful life. The solution to most challenges demands disciplined or self control not only prayers and fasting. ***Anyone who spends all their earnings to live in debt just to impress another person lacks discipline.***

Be faithful in small things.

TIP 97

MOVE IN DIRECTION OF the clock. Unless a clock is faulty, it keeps moving forward. Your time is your life, and as it keeps ticking away, you can't stop it, but you can invest, use, or waste it. Those who live to please people are the worst time wasters. Your time is the greatest asset you have to drive your success in life. Learn to convert every second of your life into a useful product, and you will be on your way to endless wealth. Everyone who thinks they have time, waste time the most because as they procrastinate, the time is ticking away. *Time is the universal asset given to man which qualifies everyone, regardless of religion, to prosper on Earth. It all depends on our understanding of it*.

Keep reaching out & touching lives.

TIP 98

GIVE TO THE NEEDY. Helping others in need is the best way to make your day count. Being kind to others makes you feel good and enhances your health because it brings joy to the heart. A man you successfully lift from the pit might end up lifting many people tomorrow. Every act of kindness will help to brighten the day of someone. **Daily add value through kindness; it is a gift that anyone who is willing can afford to give.**

Godliness in character makes a great leader.

TIP 99

STOP RUNNING FROM YOUR challenges. Have the understanding that, as we live, there will always be one challenge or another. Learn to face your challenges and prepare to resist them with counteractions and wisdom. Anything that is not contributing to your success or peace of mind should be resisted consciously. A challenge will either make us better or worse depending on our mindset toward it, and it can possibly lead us to our helpers. **The reason for every long-time crisis is the lack of wisdom and courage to face our fear or challenges. Criticize yourself to find solutions to your challenges, but never condemn yourself.**

If you want success, look for a problem to solve.

TIP 100

READ BOOKS AND ATTEND seminars. The treasures of life are hidden in books. If you need solutions or answers to solve some problems, take the time to get relevant books that address such a problem. Attend seminars to learn from others and interact for more knowledge. You can't sufficiently learn within yourself. No one has the monopoly on knowledge or wisdom. Study to show yourself approved unto God. *A good reader is a leader and an addicted reader is a great leader—read daily to increase your capacity to positively influence your world.*

Only you can stop you.

TIP 101

LOVE YOUR NEIGHBORS AS yourself. The love you have toward others will be the drive that moves you to contribute more to society. A life of positive impact is a life of love. It will plant a sense of urgency to daily add value to any family, organization, group or nation in which you find yourself. Love dispels hate. *Extend your love to let the expression of your love heal the wounds of the hopeless in your community as much as you can.*

Keep on moving on!

101 GOLDEN TIPS
Making Your Day Count

Our time is our life and as each second ticks away, so our life is ticking away. We must be wise to make each day count by productively converting every minute into products that will account for the essence of our living.

The tips in this book are for you. Read, understand, and practice them in order to make each day of your living be a blessing to your generation.

A Publication of World Leadership & Inspirational Foundation.

WORLD LEADERSHIP AND INSPIRATIONAL FOUNDATION.

WORLD LEADERSHIP AND INSPIRATIONAL FOUNDATION was registered as a nonprofit, tax-exempt 501© (3) organization in Massachusetts. It is a Foundation with the primary aim of raising responsible Ambassadors that will help power and extend the spiritual and positive social growth in our communities across the world. We teach, coach, mentor and educate minds to direct them toward being a positive contributor or finding solutions to problems in the society. We are accomplishing these assignments through the help of God and support from our partners who share in our vision that the world is in dare need of responsible Ambassadors in every facet of life to make it a better place for all. Every nation needs the positive contributions of her citizens to achieve her goals hence, we are out to contribute our quota as a complement to government efforts across the world through mind development.

A copy purchased of this book is an indirect support for our vision in building the minds of our tomorrow leaders toward finding solutions to the world's problems and extending act of kindness to the less priviledge across the world..

You can reach out to us at wordlight@yahoo.com or visit us at www.wordoflight.net for any further enquiries. Thanks.

CPSIA information can be obtained
at www.ICGtesting.com
Printed in the USA
BVHW081214250219
541082BV00010B/1492/P

9 781946 453495